SUM

SUM

poems

ZACHARIAH WELLS

BIBLIOASIS • WINDSOR, ONTARIO

FIRST EDITION

Library and Archives Canada Cataloguing in Publication

Wells, Zachariah, 1976-, author
Sum / Zachariah Wells.

Poems.
Issued in print and electronic formats.
ISBN 978-1-77196-030-4 (pbk.).--ISBN 978-1-77196-031-1 (ebook)

I. Title.

PS8645.E458S94 2015 C811'.6 C2014-907963-X
C2014-907964-8

Biblioasis acknowledges the ongoing financial support of the Government of Canada through the Canada Council for the Arts, Canadian Heritage, the Canada Book Fund; and the Government of Ontario through the Ontario Arts Council and the Ontario Media Development Corporation.

Canada Council for the Arts Conseil des Arts du Canada
Canadian Heritage Patrimoine canadien
ONTARIO ARTS COUNCIL CONSEIL DES ARTS DE L'ONTARIO
50 YEARS OF ONTARIO GOVERNMENT SUPPORT OF THE ARTS
50 ANS DE SOUTIEN DU GOUVERNEMENT DE L'ONTARIO AUX ARTS

Edited by Carmine Starnino
Copy-edited by Emily Donaldson
Typeset and designed by Kate Hargreaves

PRINTED AND BOUND IN CANADA

for Rachel

Each of us is various, many people, a prolixity of selves. Which is why the person who disdains his world is not the same as the person who rejoices or suffers because of his world. In the vast colony of our being there are many species of people, thinking and feeling differently.

—Fernando Pessoa/Bernardo Soares

EGO

I am the lord, the thief and the vassal
Water, I morph to fill any vessel
Wherever I am, I speak like a local

I sift like ash through grates and then settle
I mimic and ape; I'm brash and I'm subtle
I'm an alloy forged from ten thousand metals

I am the stove, the pot and the kettle
I patch over holes like plaster and spackle
I am the block and I am the tackle

I am a torrent and I am a trickle
I am the treacherous course through a tickle

I am most busy when I am most idle
I am the whip, the bit and the bridle

I am the bolt, the hinge and the knuckle
I am a belt in search of its buckle

I am the stamen, the pistil, the petal
I am the jot and I am the tittle
I'm obliging, yes, but no one's lickspittle

I'm jackpine, catspruce, cedar and maple
I am the stake, the stitch and the staple
I am the storm, the stallion, the stable

I can cram worlds in the cup of a thimble
I'm gauche and immodest; I'm shy and I'm humble

I am fraught silence preceding a battle
I am the fang and I am the rattle

I am the Talmud and I am the Bible
I am all manner of slander and libel

I have been Cain and I have been Abel
I am the feast and I am the table
I am the dirge of the Tower of Babel

I'd speak the truth, but I doubt that I'm able

after Robert Graves

1

BROKEN ARROW

Only there is Now. There is no
Then and When. How Zen. How then
know We when to show
ourselves? Our Selves: those little Men

inside our Minds machining
Time, fabricating patchwork panes
to stitch and mount in a montage of what We've seen—
bad grammar: *We see,* that should be. Oh, the pains

We take to stake a claim on Space.
Such a queer little race.

after Brian Greene

MOTHS AND MEN

You'd swear she was made for self-immolation
the way she spirals onto ad hoc pyres
—bonfires, candlewicks, shivaree mobs—
but crossed wires
is what prompts the moth to tithe herself
to some lunatic church. Delve
deeper: what misfires
is an elegant compass to which stars
and moon, optically infinite, are lodestone
of a luminate sort: their glow,
shed on her eyes' arrayed guides, shows
the moth home. Rays shone
in spikes, like spokes from a hub,
draw her to headlights, autos-da-fé, torches:
the moth's led astray by our radiant porches.

after Richard Dawkins

A SPANDREL IN THE WORKS

for Stephen Jay Gould

Should you wish to span the gap between fact
and fact, why not slap a handy spandrel—
the ornamented panel between an arch
and its right-angled box—on the spot?

It slots so neatly, like a spanner
in the gears of a clock. Stare long enough
at the air beneath the string of a stair
(where we store buckets, brooms and excess stuff

—unless a second stair's secreted there),
or at the circumflected hats about
the peg (round) in the hole (square)
that indicate an absent "s" and tell

us how and where to stress a vowel's sound,
and you're bound to have ideas expand
and spread into spearheads arrowed,
albeit off-mark, straight at the bowels

of this perplexus. So what if they bounce
back? So what if what they posit's merely
nominal, noumenal, epiphenomenal?
So what if it's a scoundrel's tack

which does nothing so much as explain
the by-catch of your hypertrophic brain?

TO THE BLOBFISH

With that glum grimace and globular
schnozz, to say nought of a slimy bod
aquiver on trawler deckboards as though plopped
untimely from a jello mold, you're not

exactly what I'd call grace embodied.
Wanting the spines and fangs of deep-sea monsters,
sporting no luminous bulbs or underslung jaw,
you scupper our awe. We see you and go *awwww,*

what a sadsack. Scrawled on that only-a-ma
mug—gasping on alien oxygen
following a four hundred fathom haul
from the niche in which you're fittest—is a law:

in the dark, you won't need a pretty face;
those pressures refine the idea of grace.

THE TITLE TRACK

The title track was a huge hit,
but anything the artist says is art,
is art; avant-garde

is nothing natural, but nevertheless
there are biotic defaults.
It is a cool lyric,

BUT it is direct quotation. If you want
some kind of sterile politically correct
... But I'm glad to stop. Having a career

in art is boring. Nature is trying
to kill you and offers nothing but snow:
the entire digital pro-

cess. Nothing groundbreaking here.
Why search for an experience?
The vocals are bordering on obnoxious,

lazy, self-hating. The developments
described above are attractive,
produced by chance or intuition

as we know from our experience
of Darkcore era Jungle. Yuppies
who think they're hip

should dissolve the boring
ones. I would know nothing
about classical music had I not become a church

that allowed it to happen,
from which furs and fish
may well have had to resist. Heaven

is a place where nothing happens.
But what's the alternative? Such dreary
zombies have nothing to say but insist,

using breakbeats, lunatic
rapping, a stunning progressive
rock album. Aliens might have left messages

in the "junk DNA." Even if it comes
with the anguished knowledge that nothing
produced is real, it is this very quality

that endears it to a minor Italian group. The problem
is they don't produce even average
quality papers with a lot

of "names," but they keep you
capable of being well set. But now, the question
of technique is confused by deliberate

noodling to erect a sound platform with virtues
or ethics. The poor should shut up
today's paid obtuse idiot

who knows nothing, but loves to pretend.
A radical paring down to no-nonsense fundamentals,
it becomes boring and weak, just words

proliferating. Deployment
of Cruise missiles made banality
blue chip, pornography

avant-garde, and tchotchkes into trophy
art. By the end of the poem, there is the glowing cactus.
Call it experimentation

if you will, but the simple truth is that I have been
obsessed with how boring the jungle would be
if the crickets and birds were always successful.

But that's another topic. It's nothing but a joke.

BIOGRAPHY OF A YARDLONG SPIKE

After the sparked powder
shot the tamping iron up
like a javelin through

cheekbone, brain and out
the crown of Phineas
Gage, it should surprise no one

that "Gage was no longer
Gage." Less often
noted is how this freak

occurrence rewrote
the story of that spike.
Far from inanimate, the tool

became, in a flash of lit
powder, Phin's drunken
father, the mother who

never spoke love, teachers
who said he'd go nowhere,
the priest who swapped candy

for favours, the best friend
who stole his girl and each
and every broad who said

no. The spike became
fourth-quarter fumbles
and locker room taunts,

his alienation from labour
and nature and man. It was
the stylus that scratched

dark, indelible signs
on the blank page of poor,
poor Phineas Gage.

ANATTĀ

Sorry, I'm not myself today. Lately,

    I think I never am. I was yesterday

beside myself and from that angle

    I could see the cracks and fissures,

the stitches and seams. So it seems

    this swarming hive of cells—each a self

that buds and blossoms and browns—

    has some unified purpose, but fact is

they're merely consigned to a cubicled

    lifetime, till they die and return for more

of the same. And so I am reborn,

    even before I'm buried and broken

down into dirt. If today I'm not myself,

    it's because I'm busy being everything else.

after David Weisman

TO THE SUPERB LYREBIRD

Mountebank dancer and manic mimic,
    is there a bush ruckus your syrinx can't clone?
Bubbly corkpops and glassclinks at picnics;
    kookaburra's cackle when its cover is blown;
    alarm panic, siren wail, chainsaw drone;
motor drive's whirr and aperture's click
as it captures your likeness; trigger-snick
    and barrel blast of the shot that missed home;
honey-eaters' chitter and moth-wings' flutter;
    snoring koalas and colicky babies;
    the lunatic howl of a dingo with rabies;
wind-bang stutter of a torn-loose shutter;
        all the ringtones of a cellular phone—
        no song you can't sing, but no song your own.

after David Attenborough

CHOOSE YOUR OWN DEBENTURE

Would I be doing *x* if not for *y*?
Fucked if I know. Can't imagine why
not, but then neither can I stir the cream
and sugar from my coffee. The disinterest

rate is indexed to entropic dégrin-
golade and life is but a lucid dream—
you can change the outcome on the fly,
but it takes absurdly rigid discipline.

2

DREAM MACHINE

I set the dream machine in motion
and closed my eyes to see what shapes emerge
on the cave walls of my eyelids in the
stroboscopic flicker of its spin.

I closed my eyes to see what shapes emerge,
but nothing coalesced in the rhythmic,
stroboscopic flicker of its spin.
I dozed off, the dream machine still running,

and no forms coalesced in the thermic
welter of my sleep. I had a dream that
I dozed off, the dream machine still running,
and that it showed me things I couldn't see

in the welter of my waking. I had a dream that
a scorched fox emerged from a forest fire
and showed me things I couldn't see
were killing him. I woke. From the flicker

a scorched fox emerged. From the fire
a voice was speaking. It told me that
we're killing him. I woke. From the flicker
of the dream machine, I saw nothing,

but a voice was speaking. It told me that
I had to look beyond the patterns
of the dream machine. I saw nothing
but the wavelengths of its light.

after Ted Hughes

PROSCENIUM

I know nothing of the role I play.
Rolling over, I raise a middle finger to the day
whose sunlight splits the window's slats
and pounds me with its brickbats
and reproofs. This is proof that I exist
despite the fact the timepiece on my wrist
no longer ticks and the calendar page
has read September since I can't remember when. Rage
against the coming of the light gets you
nowhere fast, but the blood it sets asimmer lets you
feel a little something. From the parlour comes
the rhubarb-rhubarb fizz of conversation, drums
rumble in the pit, I rise and shuffle into the day,
knowing nothing of the role I play.

after Wisława Szymborska

VASOPRESSIN

The prairie vole's a faithful mate,
the montane vole a man-whore,

but jigger with the latter's genes
just so, so vasopressin

secreted during sex hits
receptors in the neural

sweet spot, and the egregious slut
becomes a prairie home

companion, never more
to heed his pecker's wanton

will. Vasopressin is an anti-
diuretic; a scrip will help

recidivist pissabeds
keep their duvets dry

at night. I have a soft spot
for certain diuretics that tickle

my brain's pleasure domes and make me
prone to indiscretions. I get

no buzz from steady love.
Perhaps a hormone dose or some

slick shuffle of my chromosomes
would fix me up and keep me

out of trouble. Maybe then
I'd be the man you always wanted.

after David Eagleman

LOVE SONG: THOU ALONE

And if I pay out sufficient
cordage, will you hang
yourself? By Christ, I'm tired
of the self-dramatics
of martyr-complex men. Get off
the cross, Alan, your lot's no worse
to bear than any other's—
unless it be mine to live
with a self-despising fool
like you. No, as attractive
as the offer to join you
in your shack of hazards is,
I'll have to pass. Get your
shit together, man, contract
what you can't do yourself,
tame that rage, straighten
what is bent, then call me
and we'll talk. Until then,
I've better things to do
than cater to the vanity
of men. If you're so stupid
as to pin your southpaw
to the cross, I'm not the one
to nail the right, nor will I
pull the spike out with the claw,
but leave you dangling there
until your weight undoes
your work and you're left lying
in the sawdust to lick
your blessed wound.

after Alan Dugan

SUNK COSTS

The fact that I persist despite the futile
nature of this brutal quest is no
proof that I want reason. If bloated
bait lingers on my line and I hammer stakes
three fingers deeper into carbonized
humus, you must not see me as apostle
to St. Anthony, follower of fool's
errands or keeper of extinguished flames.
Caeteris paribus et mutatis mutandis,
if I don't brake or bail, it's because I can't
go on, but, like Sisyphus who is,
of course, just like the rest of us, I must.
Now is no time to reckon or cut loss—
now is when I must honour my sunk costs.

after Daniel Kahneman

ACHROMATOPE

The accident killed my sense of colour;
the world developed as a muddled, duller
place. Not black and white, not sepia flushed,
not even grayscale—as if God had crushed
the universe, squeezed out the juice and zest,
left nothing but a husk. If I were pressed
to put words to it, I'd say *sick*, *impure*,
dirty, *distressed*—but all that I was sure
of was that everything had changed. I lost
my taste for favourite foods (tomatoes grossed
me out—green or red, they all smelled black);
every love I had became a loss, a lack.
I even lost my fervid urge for sex—
I couldn't stand the sight of human flesh,
its hazy-pale and waxen hues of death.
Add to that the fact my field of depth
got skewed: every shadow took on form,
each pavement crack turned obstacle. Deformed,
all twisted, warped, deformed. I tried to paint
as I once did, but images came out faint
and indistinct to eyes with normal sight.
Blinded by bare bulbs, blinking in sunlight,
I withdrew from the world that I had known,
my last tint vestiges turned monochrome—
I embraced the weirdness of my plight
and got myself acquainted with the night.
In these dark arts, I became a master
bent on hauling booty from the disaster
of my shipwrecked sight. I'd sleep days,
wake to wander streets soaked in the rays
of sodium lamps, that whitewash I hated
for the way it would rape and desecrate
the rainbow—but now, it made my vision
sharper. I had never with such precision

been able to pinpoint detail, could read, say,
a license plate four hundred yards away.
I returned to canvas with fresh vigour,
my palette smaller, my purpose bigger,
toiling fifteen or sixteen hours a day
to translate my pain in this innovated way.
To my surprise, there developed a craze
for the works of my "black and white phase."
To the patrons trawling the gallery
at a vernissage, my affliction was unknown,
my green specs a trick perhaps to hide stoned
eyes. What they don't know pays my salary,
the hurts I've suffered are clandestine
and I possess a strength they can't imagine.
A doctor wrote to say he had a cure
for my condition. I politely demurred.
I now see the light as it exists: in waves,
not those tinted shadows in Plato's cave,
and will suffer no mortal fool to lift
the veil of my dark paradoxical gift.

after Oliver Sacks

HYDE

I am your genius
your nightmare
unlocked

preverbal pure animal
pop
I uncork you

I disown you
like a filthy robe
I dethrone you

I am will
unclouded by doubt's
brown shadow

I am what you know
you did
in the night

I clone you

I am ego
surrendered
to id's sheer quiddity

I know
no stupidity
no moral, no code

I have ripped
off the lid
and shown you

BROKEN

Broken again. Again I lie broken
by barley and far. A corvid croaking
draws dawn from behind ocean's smoking
horizon. Moon, that grimy old token,
clatters into its slot. No word spoken
now could cradle my aching, no cloaking
device keep in the raw wattage poking
beams through my stitches. I've been awoken
nights—more than I can name—by your breath's pause
and lain with my ear to your mouth, love.
With others and others I'd lie before you,
broken, awake, but bound by no laws,
I'd steal out, my departure a lie of
omission—even words left unspoken aren't true.

MENTAL MOONSHINE

My braincase is prinked with pinpricks of stars
and stinks of the fetid toes of the dead.
My brainflower blows its little green head;
bloodied bull, dips horns to carve scars

in the dirt. In a humming ditch, those *soirs*
doux have died slowly, plashing and red.
My braincase is prinked with pinpricks of stars
and stinks of the fetid toes of the dead.

My brain, a train of vagabond boxcars,
discharges its gold-plated freight of lead
bars, chugs from the barrens, deadheads
it to cloud-locked Valhallas of stars.

My braincase floods with the light of dead stars.

after Émile Nelligan

3

UNDERWHELMED, IF THAT'S A WORD

I'd say the book was disappointing,
but I had no expectations
of its excellence, so that would be
misleading. I'd say my team's performance
fails to satisfy, but its salary
and management point to precisely
such a mediocre season. I'd complain
about the weeds that choke my garden,
but their presence is testament to my
indifferent stewardship. I'd say inadequate
is not the aptest word to summarise
the manifest insufficiencies
of life here as we know it, but I
can think of nothing better at the moment.

after Sloan

MAGIC MAN

to John McDonald

I caught this morning's highlight reel sens-
ation, sensei of the second sack, prime
pivot's dazzle and dash, flop, flip, quicklime-,
grass- and dirt-grimed shirt, shy grin flashed, defence
maestro catching all comers like a chainlink fence.
No gilding for his great glove in this high time
of silver slugging guildsmen, but, oh, sublime
the achieve of, the mastery of our diamond prince!

Consigned to ride pine for lack of thunder
in his bat, no grievance, gripe, no slack-
sailed slump drags that verve, craft, hustle under.
No less we've come to expect, Johnny Mac,
and yet we gasp, goggle and, awed, wonder
how you render routine the miraculous act.

after Gerard Manley Hopkins

AN ENGINEER PONDERS INTELLIGENT DESIGN

The eye, they say, look at the eye, nothing
so complex could've come by hap,
would be like a tornado northing
through a boneyard, assembling a Boeing from scraps.

Well sir, I never yet seen God devise jets
and as for optics, I've made better goggles
for robots. If what we got's good as it gets,
how come I see so many glass lenses?

Nearsighted, farsighted, astigmatic,
crosseyed, walleyed, colour blind, macular
degeneration, glaucoma, cataracts—
that the suckers *ever* work's miraculous,

considering they got inserted upside-down!
And don't get me started on the wiring,
so cocked-up and crufty, it'd take a town
of neurologists to map its misfiring

matrix of circuits and switches. And let's
not forget the extra bits: appendix,
gall bladder, supernumerary digits—
you'd swear a committee of idiots

drew up this blueprint. But give credit
where credit's due: two kidneys and two lungs
make uncommon sense in the event
of malfunction, and you'd not want one tongue

more in your head, but Christ, why only one
pump to move blood and one filter to clean it?
A single engine's dandy for a half-tonne
pickup, but you need at least two on a jet!

And then there's the sinus and spine,
chronic pain wherein's a constant reminder
they'd much rather their maker'd aligned
them with the ground. You've got to wear blinders

if you're to miss the sheer nonsense
of imputing such a bloody botch to design.
If I'd Frankensteined this unholy mess,
my son—well sir, I'd just have to resign!

SQUALID

Squalid always spools my thoughts to seagulls,
filthy squallers that they are—like that one,
swooping down to send the starlings squawking
off their supper on the lawn—which gives me
pause, recalling as I do the dollars
squandered down urinal drains in bars
of dubious repute and the blotto
fucks that followed ugly hour's migraine
wattage—which makes me think (despite myself)
of babies and bad weather and water
drops dripping through roof thatch to puddle
in a dark corner of a daub and wattle
hut—and so my thoughts sprawl out to all
the soiled, the poor, the crawling, stolid
things this planet stores and harbours from the storm
and void—and then contract to rest (or stall)
on the scroll of sordid squibs that I have scrawled.

THE PARKINSONIAN REFLEXOLOGIST

People who live by a pen
mightier than the sword beaten
into a ploughshare don't share
their secrets lightly. You can't
make a silk purse from pigs in a blanket
no matter how well
you porkbarrel over the falls.
If you get caught fucking the dog,
deny the devil his Scooby Doo.
You've got to give 110% of your ass
on the line if you want to get in line
for tough loving. It's hard to get head
when your ball's in the bunker
and your club is a spade.
Stupid is as smart phones; my darling
is an open netbook, a bitter tablet
to spit or swallow. That fish
out of water is off the hook
and into the line of fire. Dead men
don't chase their own tails
down blind alleys. If I wanted your vice
I'd bust my balls to live by the sweat
off my bag. Wall to wall shagging
leads to black eyes and blots
on the bottom line. At the end of the day
another day comes knocking. Seize
the dayjob you won't quit
and throttle it to within an inch
of your wife. Pull all the stops
out of the dike and throw away
the keynote address. Dressing for success
is bound to fail the acid test
so don't sweat the small stuff

in your boxers or briefs
if you can't get it up the garden path.
Go hang your twisted knickers in the wind.

after Dodds, Dewdney & Muldoon

ONE AND ONE

For every one there is a one, and one
and one make one, divided.

For every one a one must die, and every
death is one, provided

every other is a one and one
is every other.

An other and a one make one,
husbanded and brided.

The union of a one and one
makes other, suicided.

Self-murder of the one-in-one is mother
of the other one and one

another's one-in-ones conspire to smother
other ones, while lovers

wire their one and ones
implacably together.

One is bound and gagged by one, one
saws and frays the knot

of one, and one
lets slip the tether.

after George Herbert

THE WOUND

It didn't bleed, but would seep a bit of lymph
on Sundays. It could be kept covered
by clothes, but liked to be exposed as much
as possible—though fresh air did little
to close it. It was a portal, a wormhole
between the time of its infliction
and infinite points in the future. It breathed,
and if, in perfect stillness, you inclined
your ear toward its puckered lips, you'd swear
it muttered in a foreign tongue. Somehow,
it staved off infection, was odourless
but for a faint floral whiff. Once, I saw
a hummingbird moth hover above it,
then bury her proboscis deep in the folds.

NOISE

I don't know if it's awol during daylight hours
or if the tinnitus in my left ear is merely
dimmer when I'm out and about my business,
its whine drowned in the din of city traffic
so I forget it's there until, horizontal
in the dark, I'm ready to receive it. Or, like now,
it makes its nuisance presence known when I sit
before a blank screen wondering what to write.

I can't pinpoint when my little hum got going,
don't know if it's grown louder or if one day
it just fluttered down and lit upon my shoulder,
singing. It's probably the product of imperfect
employment of ear defenders on airport tarmacs
and in the thrumming innards of the Hawkers
I offloaded. I remember landing in Hall Beach
one summer day and, once the prop stopped spinning,
I cracked the cargo hatch to such an immaculate
bare flash of silence that I half wondered if I'd been
struck deaf—until Jonah fired up the forklift
and rumbled up to greet us. Flying home, I sat
mid-cabin in the empty '48, chanting
Dylan Thomas poems aloud, thinking
that the pilots wouldn't hear me with their headsets on,
over the racket of those twin Rolls Royce Darts
I'd parked myself between.

And then there was the neighbour
who heard me, through the wall we shared, reading
Horace in the wee hours and asked me, awkwardly,
if I *prayed* at night.

And were the voices that I heard
as I lay abed in Resolute Bay the dark
season hallucinations of a man left
too much alone by the shore of the Northwest Passage—
or signals picked up by my fillings? I listed
to the static of the HF radio enough
to know the tricks the magnetosphere plays on the ear.

John Cage, in his quest for perfect silence, encased
himself in an anechoic chamber, only
to experience the flow and sizzle of his
blood and nerves as auricular phenomena.

I once tried unsuccessfully to give a message
to a woman on a train, until, looking up
from her book, she switched her hearing aid on. "Sorry,"
she said, "I prefer to hear nothing when I read."
Naively, I've since caught myself at odd times
envying that option, prone to distraction
as I am—but then it strikes me that this intermittent
buzzing could be my frequency among the quick.

RYE

Rye renders me horny. Nothing wry
about its muzzy fisheye lens,
through which I can see all the fuckers stunting
to fight me. Call it X-rye. Call it men's
intuition. Call it a kickstart
to the dry-seized engine of a heart
in a body propped up on blocks, shunting
late-night freights of blood from the yard
to all my peripheral parts. It makes me
unbearably sad. It makes me unable,
even as it digs in the spurs. Listen:
I need you now. I'm under the table
with supernova stars in my eyes. Take me
home before they burn out. I'll miss them.

BAFFLE

When every little scent's intense, intensity
itself grows tedious. Not all sensations
can be sensational should one remain

whole and sane. Holy thoughts and sacred
sentiments must be consigned to holidays
where they belong, so that the mundane

and unremarkable might also grow.
I know a woman who can hear an ant
worrying a seed deep within a fissure

on a beam. This doesn't lead to rapture—
it causes pain. I take a walk around
the garden walls I've built as baffle

to the fascinating marvels of my life.

I

Such a slim barrow into which to stuff
        a life; such a narrow beam to cross
    and brace the walls. Pollarded and shallow-
        rooted, it resists the winds, persists
despite its pruning. Stiff and stolid
        in its ramrod stance, it stands, but shifts
    and strays when no one's watching. It sees
        the road ahead, but is always looking
back. It asserts and it equivocates.
        It makes mistakes. It flirts with grief and grace.
    It wears a mask to hide its missing face.

after Erving Goffman

ACKNOWLEDGEMENTS

Versions of these poems, sometimes under different titles, have appeared in the following:

Approaches to Poetry: The Pre-Poem Moment (Frog Hollow Press); *Baffle* (Baseline Press); *The Best Canadian Poetry (Tightrope Press, 2010 & 2012); Contemporary Verse 2; Encore; Event; The Fiddlehead; Forget; FreeFall; The Humber Literary Review; Ludicrous Parole* (Mercutio Press); *The New Quarterly; Partisan; Poems from Planet Earth* (Leaf Press); *Poetry'zown; Riddle Fence; This; The Toronto Review of Books; The Walrus; The Winnipeg Review.*

An earlier version of "Achromatope" was published as a limited edition broadside by Frog Hollow Press in 2007.

"Broken," "Anattā," and "I" were set to music by composer Erik Ross, as part of the song cycle "Waypoints," which was performed by baritone Phillip Addis and pianist Emily Hamper at live recitals in Toronto, Paris and Montreal in 2013 and 2014. These three poems, along with a fourth ("Waypoints"), were privately printed as a limited edition commemorative broadside by Andrew Steeves of Gaspereau Press. With the help of crowdfunding, the author was able to attend the recital at the Opéra Bastille in Paris and would like to thank everyone who contributed to the campaign, especially James Calhoun, Trevor Owen, Mark Rieger, Karyn Sullivan, Sarah Trend, and Francis Wooby.

The author acknowledges the support of the Canada Council for the Arts, Arts Nova Scotia and the University of New Brunswick.